Python:
A Step by Step
for Beginners

Disclaimer and Terms of Use:

Effort has been made to ensure that the information in this book is accurate and complete, however, the author and the publisher do not warrant the accuracy of the information, text and graphics contained within the book due to the rapidly changing nature of science, research, known and unknown facts and internet. The Author and the publisher do not hold any responsibility for errors, omissions or contrary interpretation of the subject matter herein. This book is presented solely for motivational and informational purposes only.

Table of Contents

Introduction

Our life mainly revolves around computers, from everyday chores to the most minute things. A few examples are communication, transportation and media, since the world is one large global network. One can say we have become so prone to it that it's almost impossible to go on living without actually dabbling in this field. For all those dabblers out there, this might just be what you have been in search for! Are you a newbie in the field of technology and coding? Or tired of going through numerous tutorials and guidebooks on how to read Python language? Well your search has just ended because this guide is the perfect tool book for you.

Python is a very popular high-level programming language, which pay specific focus to code readability. Most of the statements in Python are like plain English, and this language also allows you to do more things in lesser lines of code than in languages such as C++ and Java. Python has a dynamic type system, automatic memory management, and something that proves to come in *very* handy: a large standard library. Python is generally a very popular learning language when it comes to dealing with machine learning projects.

This book is one that can prove to be useful for you if you want to learn Python, regardless of whether you're a newbie or a pro to the world of programming. Every concept has been explained with a little introduction before moving on to how it is implemented in Python, and what things you need to keep an eye out for. These introductions to concepts are not VERY detailed as so to appear cumbersome, although experienced programmers can simply skip those parts if they want to.

This book also contains code samples, as so to better illustrate the concept. Readers are advised to write those same codes (or codes similar to them) at least once on their own, it will help them get a great understanding of the language early on.

We start right from the basics about how to deal with this language and how to go on about it. Specifically, how to install Python on your system and get it up and running. From there, we move on to the fundamentals of a programming language, concepts that you should be familiar with if you have studied any programming language before. Elaborating how those concepts work in Python will give you a clear and proper understanding of this language, and will equip you enough to start working on it right away. From there on out, we move on to more advanced concepts.

Even if you're new to programming, this book will take you through it as smooth as possible. The thing about Python is that it's an easy language even for beginners so you have nothing to worry about it. Most operating systems mainly such as Linux come with an installed Python but if it's not on your computer, there's no need to worry, for we've got it covered! Of course by no time, we can assure you that you will be an expert.

Chapter 1: Python 2 and Python 3: What's the difference?

Straight off the bat, the first thing that you should know about Python is the fact that there are two versions of Python: Python 2.x and Python 3.x. The latest version of Python 2 is Python 2.7.10, and the latest version of Python 3 is Python 3.5.0. In simple words, Python 2 is the past, and Python 3 is both the present and future of the language.

What this statement means is that Python 2 is old, and will no longer see any major releases. Work on Python 2.x has stopped, whereas Python 3.x is under active development and has already seen several stable releases.

But what's the difference between these two versions? Well, here are some of the differences between the two languages:

The print statement

The print statement has a different syntax in both versions. This has been elaborated in a later chapter as well. The difference isn't huge; it's basically the required presence and optional presence of brackets. Here's how it is:

For Python 2.x:

print "I am computer"

print("I am computer")

Both statements work fine in Python 2.x. However in Python 3.x, only the latter is admissible. That is, for Python 3.x:

print("I am computer")

Brackets in the print statement are absolutely necessary in Python 3.x, and raise a syntax error if omitted. It's one of the most frequent mistakes that programmers make when writing a code in Python 3.x after years of development experience in Python 2.x, so this is something you need to remember. Brackets bring necessary add a nice touch, if I am to add a personal preference, since it makes it appear as a proper function.

Integer division

Suppose you're dividing two integers. Logically, the answer you will get should also be an integer. If you want the answer in float, you will have to cast the result to float. After all, that's how it is in Java! That's also how it is in Python 2.x... But not in Python 3.x.

Consider the following piece of code:

print(3/2)

Here's the output in Python 2.x: 1

Here's the output in Python 3.x: 1.5

So you see, dividing two integers can give a float result if you get a decimal value as the answer.

User inputs

Often it happens that we need the user to enter an input via the keyboard. It could be a string, a number, or anything else. In Python 2.x, we have two statements for that. One stores the input as an integer, and the other as a string.

My_input = input("Enter a number please: ")
Type:Integer

My_input = raw_input("Enter a number please: ")
      Type:String

After execution of the first line, the type of the variable 'My_input' shall be integer. Whereas the after execution of the second line of code, the type of the variable 'My_input' shall be string.

In Python 3.x however, there is no 'raw_input' statement. There is only the 'input' statement, and it always stores the result as a string. It can later be cast to an integer if need be.

My_input = input("Enter a number please: ")
      Type:String

Other differences

Apart from the abovementioned ones, there are some other differences between Python 2.x and Python 3.x as well, such as the xrange function, Unicode, rasing and handling exception etc. However, we shall not elaborate on those in this book. You can find information on these differences easily enough on the internet. Rest assured, the differences mentioned above should be enough to get you started on Python, and shall also help you if you ever find yourself experiencing the need to port code from Python 2.x to Python 3.x.

Chapter 2: Installing and Running Python

So obviously, the first thing that you'll need to do to get started is to install Python on your system, whichever version of it that you fancy. It is quite easy and simple to install Python.

For Windows

To install Python on Windows, go to the official website of Python: www.python.org. From here, you can download the latest release of Python. You can find both versions here, Python 2.x and Python 3.x. The latest version of Python 2 is Python 2.7.10, and the latest version of Python 3 is 3.5.0.

Once you have downloaded the required version of Python, simply double click the installation file, follow the instructions and you shall have Python installed on your system!

By default, Python would install to a directory such as C:\Python 27 if you're installing Python 2.7, or similarly for Python 3.x. You would need to modify the PATH environment variable in order to avoid typing the full path name for a Python interpreter every time. To do so, add the following statement to your system's PATH environment variable:

C:\Python27;C:\Python27\Scripts

And likewise in the case of Python 3.x too.

For Linux

To install Python on Linux is fairly easier; if you use the terminal for it. Many Linux packages come with Python pre-installed, but nevertheless, you can install Python in your system from the terminal with this one command:

sudo apt-get install python2.7

sudo apt-get install python3.4

You can install whichever version of Python you prefer by mentioning it here, you're not only limited to Python 2.7 and 3.4! You will be prompted with a "Do you want to continue?" message; press 'y' and then the Enter key, and your system shall proceed to install the required version of Python.

Running a Python script

In order to run a Python script, you can either use the terminal, or an IDE (Integrated Development Environment). Via the terminal, it's a simple matter of navigating to the directory where the Python file is placed, and typing the following command in the terminal:

python script_name.py   For Python 2.x

python3 script_name.py   For Python 3.x

In order to run a Python script in an IDE such as PyCharm, simply open that script in the IDE, and click on the 'Run' button.

Python shell

You can also open up a Python shell in the terminal or command prompt of your system, assuming you have Python installed. To do this, simply type *python* (or *python3* for Python 3.x) in the terminal or command prompt (for Windows, Python should be added to the PATH environment variable), and a Python shell should open. Here, you can enter commands and they'll get executed one by one, as soon as you type one and press 'Enter'. This often comes in a lot of handy when you want to write a small piece of code to check something, and don't want to write a new script in a Python file or in the IDE. You shall find yourself using this more often than not once you start using Python!

Chapter 3: Writing your first "Hello, World!" program

So the first thing that anyone does while learning a new programming language is to write the basic "Hello, World!" program. It is something that gives the student a sense of accomplishment; it's a certain ritual that must be performed, if you will. Everyone writes this program first, and only after completing it does one move on to bigger and more advanced things.

Likewise, we shall do the same here. Our first step in the practical learning of Python shall be to write the "Hello, World!" program. Now, this code differs in different languages, as far as the syntax, the libraries you have to import and the nitty-gritties you have to keep an eye out for. With Python, this code is perhaps the simplest of them all, and consists of only a single line of code. It goes like this:

```
print("Hello, World!")
```

You would be wondering at this point, "That's it?", probably with an incredulous expression on your face, and the tone of the question to match. Well, I kid you not. This is actually it. For a completely baseline program such as "Hello, World!" in Python, you don't need to import any libraries, or include a main method; this shall do.

The next step shall be to save this file (make sure to keep the extension ".py", since this is the extension used for Python files), and then we shall run it through the terminal. For this, open the command prompt/linux terminal, navigate to the folder where you saved this file, and then type:

python file_name.py   (for Python 2.x)

python3 file_name.py   (for Python 3)

Alternatively, you can run this program in an IDE by simply clicking on the 'Run' button.

And voila! You should see the fateful words written on your screen, which indicate your program coming to life and saying hello to the world. Congratulations! You just wrote your first Python code!

Chapter 4: The Basics

So now that we've written our first ever Python code and executed it successfully, it's time to move on to bigger things. We shall now cover some of the basics of the Python language; vital information that you'll need in order to code using this language. If you already know programming and have coding experience in some other language, these things shall be a breeze for you, and all you'll have to keep an eye out for is the syntax. If you don't have any prior coding experience, well not to worry; we'll progress at a slow and easy pace so that you get every point.

Variables

Perhaps the most basic and paramount part of programming languages are variables. Variables in programming languages, if you don't already know, are much like the variables we study in Math; they're small containers which can hold values. So for example, you can have variables which hold integer values, or decimal values, or letter, words or sentences. There are a lot of different variable kinds available in Python, each suited to a different purpose(s). In Python, declaring variables and assigning them a value is done in a single step. Moreover, you don't need to explicitly declare what kind of a variable you're creating. Variable declaration and assignment is done like this:

myVariable = 1

Or if it's a String variable:

myVariable = "I am learning Python"

As you can see, you can pretty much create any kind of variable in Python, and you can do it the same way, since you don't have to explicitly declare what kind of a variable it is. Numeric variables are simple enough; you simply type the name of the variable, followed by an assignment operator (=) and the value, which could be an integer, or a floating point.

Strings are any collection of letters, words or sentences. Assigning strings is slightly more complex, since it involves conventions based on the type of the value. You use single quotes if the value is a single letter, double quotes if its a word, and triple quotes if its a sentence.

myString = 'a'

myString = "Look!"

myString = "'Triple quotes for a sentence!'"

You can print variables like this:

print(myString)

If you want to print a message alongside the variable value:

print("Here is my string:", myString)

There are a total of five standard data types in Python:

1. Numbers

2. Strings

3. Lists

4. Tuples

5. Dictionaries

The latter three shall be discussed later.

The print statement

The print statement in Python is quite straightforward. You don't need to import any libraries for it. The only thing to keep in mind with this statement is the difference with Python 2.x and Python 3.

For Python 3, the statement goes like this:

print("The print statement!")

print("This is some variable", some_variable)

With Python 2.x, the enclosing brackets are optional. So the above statements would work fine in Python 2.x, but so would this:

print "I am learning Python!"

The difference in syntax of the print statement is one of the prime differences between Python 2.x and Python3. Generally, it is advised to add the enclosing brackets even if you're using Python 2.x, for it increases readibility of the code, and also makes porting the code from Python 2.x to Python 3 easier.

The input statement

The input statement is also very simple. Since Python is a language which is geared towards readability and being as close to normal English as possible, there are no complications like using Scanner or creating an input stream like in Java to take user input. Simply use the following statement:

input("Any message you would like to appear: ")

You can also omit the message altogether, and simply use: input(). Upon reaching the input statement, the code will pause as it waits for the user to enter some input through the keyboard. Once the user does so and presses the 'Enter' key, the input statement returns whatever the user entered, and moves on.

If you need to do some processing on the input that the user entered, you need to save it in a variable. Here's how:

name = input("Please enter your name")

Once the user enters some input and presses 'Enter', the input shall be stored in the variable 'name', which you can then print, or use for further processing.

In Python 2.x, the input statement goes like this:

name = raw_input("Text here")

The main function

The main function is quite interesting in Python. For instance, you don't really need a main function. While in languages such as C++ and Java, you *need* a main method in which you add the block of code which will run upon execution. The main method is considered as an entry point for the application. In Python however, you cannot have a main method, and the code will still run. Obviously, it depends on the code that you're writing. If you're writing a small script for a small task, then you can omit the main method, but if you're writing a large program with many functions within the script, then it is suggested that you add a main method for readability.

The main method in Python is added in the following way:

if '__name__' == '__main__':

Sounds arduous, right? It really is. After all, "void main(void)" from C++ is a lot simpler. But this is how the main method is in Python.

One of the things to keep in mind is that there are some situations where you'll absolutely *need* to include a main method in Python. Any code *outside* of the main method gets executed before the code *inside* the main method. It's very plausible that you have some task which needs to be executed repeatedly, and you would add that in the main method. However, if for this task you need to initialize some variables and you don't want them initialized every time, then you can initialize them outside the main method. The block of code outside the main method would be executed only once, and the main method itself can be called and executed as many times as need be.

Indentation

One of the most interesting, and while we're at it, VERY important things about Python, which are what set it apart in a way from languages such as C++ and Java, is the fact that Python uses not curly or some other brackets, but rather indentation to signify the block of code that comes under a loop, conditional statement or function. Basically, loops are used to structure the language.

How does that work? Let us elaborate with an example. Suppose you have a couple of statements you want executed inside a *for* loop (don't worry about the syntax of the loop, that is covered later). Now in Java, the code would look something like this:

```
for(int i=0;i<10;i++)

{

System.out.print("We are learning Python");

System.out.print("Python is a fun language");

someVariable++;

}

System.out.print("We are outside the loop now");
```

If we were to write the same block of code in Python, it would go something like this:

```
for i in range(0, 10):

    print("We are learning Python")

    print("We are learning Python")

    someVariable+=1;

print("We are outside the loop now")
```

As you can see, to signify that a statement or block of statements must appear inside a loop, we do not use brackets, but rather indentation to do the trick. Proper indents are very important in Python, and one must keep an eye out for this. A single tab space signifies an indent. The last statement is placed the same as the *for* statement from an indentation point of view, therefore it does not appear inside the loop.

You might also have noticed that the statements in Python are not terminated with a semi-colon. This is because Python does not require a statement terminator. You can put a ; at the end of a statement if you want, it won't generate an error, but it's not necessary.

Yet another small thing to note is the fact that Python does not support post or pre-increment statements. It has to be done the other way, either as is done above, or by:

someVariable = someVariable + 1

Finally, one last thing to note in this piece of code is that the *for* loop in the Python code is followed by a colon. A conditional statement, loop statement or declaration such as that of a function or a class is always followed by a colon, and the statements that are to appear inside it are indented by one tab space.

Lists

A list in Python is, in the simplest of definitions, a collection of variables, or objects. Consider the following scenario in order to understand:

Suppose you want to write a program in which you want to store the grades of all the students in your class, entered by a user. If there is one student in your class, you'd need one variable. If, however, there are ten students in your class, you'd need ten variables to store the grades!

Declaring and initializing ten variables not only sounds like a lot of hassle, but it also makes the code very redundant and untidy. Here's how it would look like:

```python
student1 = input("Enter grade: ")

student2 = input("Enter grade: ")

student3 = input("Enter grade: ")

student4 = input("Enter grade: ")

student5 = input("Enter grade: ")

...
```

See the problem? You have the same line of code, but you're having to write it again and again because you need a different variable each time. Here is where lists come in. A list is a collection of variables under the same name. So in this scenario, you would create a list of students, and add the grades to it inside a loop. How? Before we move on to that, let's get a clearer idea of how lists work.

A list is basically a collection, and individual elements of the list are accessed through indexes. A list is always indicated with square brackets. So for example, if you have the following list:

list1 = [1,2,6,4,5,8,3]

This is a list of simple integers. To access individual elements, you would need to give the specific index of the list. So for example,

print(list1[0])

would print 1. list1[1] is 2. And so on. As you can see, the elements in a list do not begin from 1, but from 0. And therefore, the last element of this list would not be 7, but 6. A list of 10 elements would have elements ranging from 0 to 9.

You can also have a list of strings, like this:

list1 = ['red', 'blue', 'green']

A list is *dynamic*; that means that it does not have a fixed size. You can keep adding elements to it on the go. This is very useful, since in real life situations, there are a lot of scenarios where we don't exactly know the number of records we'll need to store, and therefore this dynamic nature of lists is very useful.

So if we go back to the original problem, the solution is in lists, and a very simple loop:

students = []

for i in range(0, 9):

      students.append(input("Enter marks:"))

print(students)

And there you go! Don't worry if the for loop seems confusing; it shall be covered in detail later. Also, the append function adds the object within the parentheses to the list.

Tuples

A tuple is also a collection object like a list, but there are some differences. There is a difference in syntax, for one. A tuple is declared like this:

Tuple1 = ('one',)

Tuple2 = ('one', 'two', 'three')

print(Tuple1)

print(Tuple2)

print(Tuple2[1])

The output would be something like this:

('one')

('one', 'two', 'three')

two

As you can see, individual elements of tuples are accessed much in the same way as lists. In fact, tuples so far seem almost the same as lists. So what's different?

One of the key differences between lists and tuples is the fact that tuples are immutable. An immutable object is one whose value cannot be changed once assigned. So for example, if I want to make the following addition to the above code:

Tuple2[1] = 'five'

The code shall generate an error.

This may seem like a bit of bother, and uselessness too, but immutability of objects does prove to be quite helpful in certain situations!

Dictionaries

In the most basic words, a dictionary is an object which exhibits the concept of a key-value pair. It is like a list, except that individual valuesare accessed not by indexes, but rather by keys. This is similar to the key-value pairs used in JSON objects, if you're familiar with those. Here is an example elaborating the use of dictionaries:

dict1 = {}

dict1['name'] = "Michael Harper"

dict1['age'] = 15

dict1['reg_no'] = 12543

dict1['school'] = "Beaconhouse"

As you can see, once you declare a dictionary object, you don't need to explicitly define its individual values; you can just assign values to them as if they already exist. Every entry of a dictionary has a key, and a corresponding value. Printing the dictionary would give the following result:

{'name': 'Michael Harper', 'age': 15, 'reg_no': 12543, 'school': 'Beaconhouse'}

And if you want to print individual values from the dictionary, you can do it like this:

print(dict1['school'])

You can also update an element of a dictionary. This obviously means that unlike tuples, dictionaries are not immutable.

dict1['name'] = "Almira"

You can remove all entries from a dictionary with the *clear* function, and then add new ones if you want to:

dict1.clear()

Dictionary keys have some properties which one should definitely keep in mind when using dictionaries:

- Duplicate keys are not allowed. That means that for a single key, you can only have a single value. You cannot have multiple values against the same key. If you assign a value to a dictionary element with an existing key, you are updating it, not adding another value to it. This has been elaborated with an example above.

- You can various object types as keys for a dictionary, such as integers, strings or even tuples. However, something like ['key'] is not allowed. It would generate the following error: *TypeError: list objects are unhashable.*

You can display all keys and values of a dictionary with the following methods:

dict1.keys()

dict1.values()

Finally, Python has the following built-in functions for making work with dictionaries easier:

- cmp(dict1, dict2): for comparing two dictionary objects
- len(dict1): total number of elements in the dictionary object
- str(dict1): returns a string representation of the dictionary object
- Type (dict1): returns the type of the object (dictionary object, in this case).

Importing libraries

Here's a major fundamental concept from programming languages that you might've been wondering about, assuming you're familiar with programming beforehand: How do you add libraries in your code?

For those who don't know, libraries are basically collections of similar objects that are stored for frequent use. So for example, you have a lot of different scripts in which you need to calculate the factorial of a number. So instead of writing the code of calculating the factorial of a number in each script, you write it in a library, and just import the library in your code and use the function. You can write your own libraries, and a lot of user-made libraries are also available commonly, having all sorts of functions in different domains. Importing libraries saves you a lot of time and effort!

So the question that crops up now is, how do you import a library in Python? The following statement is used for that purpose:

import codecs

Where codecs is the name of the library that we're importing. Conventionally all import statements are written at the top of the code.

Installing libraries is particularly easy in Python. While you can download the zipped file and run the setup file manually in order to install the library, a simpler way is to use pip. pip is a package management system used to install and manage libraries, or software packages that are written in Python. Once you have installed a library, you can simply import it into your code as shown above.

How to install a library using pip? Well, it's simple. It's done through the terminal, so if you're using Linux, you'll have to open up the terminal, or the Command Prompt if you're using Windows. The command goes like this:

pip install library_name

And if you're using Python3:

pip3 install library_name

You should note however, that you'll have to install the pip module before using it. Also, not all Python libraries are available for install via pip, so some you might have to install manually!

Finally, the ending note for libraries in Python is that whenever you're about to install one, make sure to check and see whether it's available for the version of Python you're using or not; that is, Python2.x or Python3. Quite often, it happens that you may install a library but when you try to import it, it generates an error because the library doesn't support the version of Python your code is in. In other words, a library may have been developed in Python 2.x and importing it in a code written in Python 3 would create an issue.

Chapter 5: Conditional Statements

If you're familiar with programming, conditional statements are something you would know like the back of your hand, so often are they used. If you're not familiar with programming, don't worry, they're EXTREMELY easy to understand and use – and very useful too!

In a nutshell, conditional statements are what the name implies: they are used to impose conditions. Through this, you can control the flow of the program. Not making a lot of sense? Don't worry, we'll explain step by step here.

So first of all, what is this 'flow of control'? Well, flow of control generally refers to the flow of execution of a code. This refers to what sections of the code are executed and what sections are not, and what sections of the code are executed repeatedly, if any. The latter part of this statement shall be explained later on in the section of loops and functions.

Consider the following scenario: Suppose that you need to write a piece of code that does something according to the kind of input that the user has entered. Like, say if entered a number between 1 and

10, you are required to calculate and display that number's factorial. And if the user enters a number between 10 and 20, you are required to calculate and display that number's square. So how would you go about it? In a broad sense of the code, you would ask the user to enter a number, and then you would check whether the number lies between 10 and 10, or 10 and 20, and then proceed accordingly.

It sounds very simple in theory. In application however, it's slightly more complex. The 'proceed accordingly' statement essentially means that you would create two separate blocks of code, one which calculates a number's factorial, and the other which calculates a number's square. And using a conditional statement, you will check whether the number lies between 1 and 10, or 10 and 20, and accordingly choose the block of code to be executed.

If-else statement

The popular if-else statement is a very basic, popular and arguably the most effective conditional statement out there. It closely models how conditions go in the English language. Suppose that a friend asks you for advice on what phone to get, and you want to tell him that if he wants productivity out of his smartphone, he should get a Windows Phone. And if he wants to be able to fully customize his smartphone from a software point of view, he should get an Android phone. If we break down this statement logically, it would look something like this:

If you want productivity, get a Windows Phone

Else, if you want customization, get an Android phone.

This is essentially how the if-else condition works in all programming languages, with minor differences of syntax of course. Obviously the syntax is slightly more rigid than the plain old English statements mentioned here, but it isn't very complex.

Let's revisit the number in ranges example, simplifying it in the process. Suppose now our requirement is that if the number entered by the user is less than 10, its factorial should be displayed. If the number is greater than 10, its square should be displayed. Using an if-else condition, here's how the code would look:

number = input("Please enter a number: ")

if number > 10:

    # code to calculate and display factorial of number

else:

    # code to calculate and display square of number

As you can see, the if condition is followed by a block of code, and so is the else condition. If the number entered is indeed less than 10 and the condition is satisfied, the block of code under the if condition would be executed, and the block of code under the else condition would be ignored. Likewise, if number entered is greater than 10 and the condition is *not* satisfied, the block of code under the if condition would be ignored, and the one under the else statement would be executed.

The inference one would make from this statement is the fact that in an if-else condition, only one block of code can be executed, because only one condition can be satisfied. It is therefore important to keep an eye on the condition you're imposing. This crops up another interesting scenario: What if we have multiple conditions?

Let's understand this with an example as well. Suppose now you have a scenario where you're calculating a student's grade from his/her percentage. If the percentage is above 90, the grade would be A+. If the percentage is between 80 and 90, the grade would be A. If the percentage is between 70 and 80, the grade would be B, and so on. We have multiple conditions here. The code in this case would look something like this:

percentage = input("Please enter the student's percentage: ")

if percentage > 90:

   grade = "A+"

elif percentage > 80:

   grade = 'A'

elif percentage > 70:

   grade = 'B'

elif percentage > 60:

```
grade = 'C'

elif percentage > 50:

    grade = 'D'

else:

    grade = 'F'
```

This may seem like a very strict marking scheme, but this is just an example. Here, *elif* basically means *else if*, and it is used in scenarios such as this one, where you need multiple conditions. An important thing to keep in mind with multiple conditions is that if one condition is satisfied, the others will be ignored. That is, the others won't be checked at all, even if they also are being satisfied. For example, in the above code, if the grade entered is 85, the second condition gets satisfied, but so do the three conditions below it; after all, 85 *is* greater than 70, 60 and 50 too! But once the second condition is satisfied, the others won't be checked, and the code will move on.

Another thing to keep in mind is that when using multiple conditions with *elif,* an *else* clause is absolutely necessary, which will dictate what should happen if none of the conditions are satisfied.

However, if there's only one condition, than an *else* clause isn't necessarily required.

Finally, the last thing to keep in mind is that you can also incorporate multiple conditions within a single *if* statement. Bringing the concept of ranges back, suppose you want to check if a number lies between 1 and 10. Now, one way to go about it would be to use nested if conditions:

if number > 0:

> *if number < 10:*

> > *#do something*

But there's a shorter and more effective to do that too, using logical operators:

If number > 0 and number < 10:

> *#do something*

Here, the logical operator *and* is sued, which means that both conditions must be true to satisfy the condition. You can also use the *or* and *not* operators.

Abbreviated if statement

There's also a shorter way of writing *if-else* statements, by essentially incorporating both if and else clauses within a single statement. This is a method usually used by experienced programmers, who want to cut down on time or/and space. The syntax is a little confusing, and it is recommended for you to familiarize yourself thoroughly with the conventional *if-else* statement before moving on to this one. The abbreviated if statement goes like this:

a = 10

b = 5

max = a if (a > b) else b

Pretty readable, no? This essentially means that the variable *max* will be assigned the value of the variable *a* if it has a greater value than the value of variable *b*. If it isn't, then *max* will be assigned the value of *b*.

Switch statement

People familiar with programming in languages such as C++, C# or Java would know of a particular switch statement. The switch statement comes in handy when you have a lot of multiple conditions, and writing the *if-else* constructs for each condition becomes a real bother. The switch statement reads the value of a single variable, and provides an easy and effective way of dealing with a lot of multiple conditions, saving space and time.

Unfortunately, Python does not have a switch statement. I don't know why, since it came in handy quiet often while dealing with a lot of multiple conditions revolving around a single scenario, but such are the grievances of Python.

Chapter 6: Loops

Loops are one of the basic and most effective components of programming languages. They make coding very easy and efficient, particularly in terms of space, and also make the code more readable. More than that, they make the life of programmers very easy, since it prevents them from rewriting code over and over again.

As with previous chapter, we'll understand the concept of loops with the help of an example as well. If you're already familiar with the concept of loops, you can skip this part.

Suppose that you're writing a piece of code where you have to print a certain statement ten times. It could be a line of asterisks, to serve as a header, or something of that sort. Now, one way to go about it would be to type the *print* statement ten times, like this:

*print("**")*

*print("**")*

*print("***
")

*print("**
")

...

However, this is a lot of wasted effort and space. Why write the same thing over and over again? This also makes the code itself come across as quite untidy and redundant. As we all know very well, necessity is the mother of invention, and thus the concept of loops was given birth to!

With loops, essentially what you can do is execute a single statement, or multiple statements, a given number of times. The statement(s) to be executed repeatedly are enclosed within the loop. In simple psuedocode, the code would look something like this:

for ten times:

*print("*************************************
*******")*

There! Now doesn't that save a whole lot of effort and space? There are multiple ways to implement loops in Python.

For loop

The *for* loop is simple and effective. It allows you to execute a given number of statements a specified number of times. The syntax goes something like this:

for loop_variable in range(1, 10):

*print("**
*******")*

As you can see, the number of times the loop should execute is specified by the *range*. The *range* is used to specify the starting and ending value for the loop, that is, what value it should start from, and after reaching what value should it end. How does it reach the end value, are you wondering? This is the beauty of *for* loops; the loop variable auto increments itself!

The loop variable is an essential part of all loops, since it keeps count. The value of the loop variable is automatically incremented by 1 at each iteration, until its value becomes equal to the ending value, at which point it stops executing.

You can also add a modification to ensure that the loop variable increments not by 1, but by 2 or some other number at each iteration. To do this, you give a third parameter to the *range* function, which is basically the step size, that is, the value by which the loop variable should increment upon each iteration.

for i in range(1, 10, 2):

    print("***")

Now this loop will run only 5 times instead of 10!

The *for* loop can also be used to iterate over lists. Here is the syntax for that:

for i in range(0, len(user_list)):

    print(user_list[i])

This simple piece of code iterates over a list and displays all its elements one by one. It is also noteworthy to mention that it is not necessary to give the starting value in the range for a *for* loop. You can simply provide an ending value, and the loop variable will iterate from 0 to that value:

for i in range(len(user_list)):

*print("*************************************
*********")*

While loop

The *while* loop is also similar in its core purpose to the for loop, but there are some differences. For instance, a *while* loop doesn't necessarily need a specified loop variable. It can operate on any variable, if one is needed. Secondly, a *while* loop doesn't automatically increment the loop variable like in the *for* loop; the increment has to be done manually. The *while* loop is generally preferred in situations when you don't' exactly how many times the loop will run, and instead want the loop to run until a certain condition is met.

To use a *for* loop to run a specific number of times, here is the syntax:

i=0

while i > 10:

*print("*************************************
*********")*

i+=1

This piece of code will print the line of asterisks 10 times.

However, the *while* loop is more useful in situations where the loop should run until a certain condition is met. Say, you want the user to enter a number, and unless that number is 5, you want to keep displaying the number, and asking him to enter a number again. In this situation, you don't exactly know the number of times the loop will run, since you don't know how many number the user will enter before he enters 5, if at all. The *while* loop comes to our rescue here:

number = input("Please enter a number: ")

while number != 5:

    print number

    number = input("Please enter a number: ")

As you can see, the loop will keep running until the specified condition is met, that is, the user enters the number 5.

Another very popular usage of the *while* loop is when you want to run an infinite loop. There are situations where you are required to implement an endless loop

– that is, the loop shall never end until and unless the user manually quits the program. This is useful for web services hosted on servers which are essentially always running and available. In such a scenario, you use the following code:

while True:

>   *# take some input, process it, and return to waiting for input stage*

You can also specify an *else* condition to a *while* loop; that is, what should happen if the condition isn't met. This is useful in scenarios where you want some piece of code to execute once the loop terminates, and only if the code within the loop was executed at least once. The syntax for that goes something like this:

while count < 10:

>   *#do something*

>   *count += 1*

else:

>   *print("Loop terminated!")*

Finally, you can also write a *while* loop as a single statement, where the syntax becomes quite similar to that of the *if* statement. This is only applicable in scenarios where the code within the loop consists of only one line.

while x > 10: print(x)

As you can see, *while* loops are a lot more flexible than *for* loops, and can allow for a variety of tasks which would be quite arduous with *for* loops.

Nested loops

Nested loops are both a menace and a blessing in the world of programming. On the outlook, they look very useful and are in fact another step in promoting code reusability, simplification and making programmers' lives easier. Nested loops essentially refer to a loop within a loop. Suppose you want to display the tables of all number from 1 to 9. This would use nested loops:

for x in range(1, 10):

   for y in range(1, 10):

      *print(x, " * ", y, " = ", x*y)*

This is how nested loops are used. As you can see, we can print the tables of all numbers from 1 to 9 up till 9 with only three lines of code using nested loops. A *for* loop can be nested within another *for* loop, a *while* loop within a *while* loop, or a *for* loop within a *while* loop or vice versa; there's no constraint.

However, nested loops are a menace in the sense that they are computationally very expensive. They essentially run for a n^2 iterations, or n*k iterations, where n is the loop variable of the first loop, and k the variable loop of the second loop. If you are a beginner when it comes to programming, this shouldn't worry you. However as you steadily move on to more advanced things, and code complexity becomes a factor that you'll have to keep in mind, then it is advised to avoid nested loops if possible, and attain the objective in some other way.

The break, continue and pass statements

Sometimes it happens that there could be more than one condition that could lead to a loop being terminated. For example, if we revisit the previous example where the user keeps entering a number and having it displayed until he enters the number 5. Suppose that now, you want to add a condition that if the user enters a negative number, the loop should terminate immediately. While this could be catered for within the *while* loop statement, we shall do it in a different way, as so to illustrate the concept of how to deal with runtime or different conditions.

There are three different statements that are used within loops: *break, continue* and *pass*. We shall examine each with an example.

- Let's start with the aforementioned scenario, where you want the loop to terminate if the user enters a negative value:

  number = input("Please enter a number: ")

  while number != 5:

      print(number)

      number = input("Please enter a number: ")

      if number < 0:

          break

Notice the *break* statement. The *berak* statement exist out of one loop. So in this scenario, if the user enters a negative number, the loop shall be terminated, even though the condition in the *while* statement hasn't been satisfied. It is also worth noticing that if you use a *break* statement in the inner loop of a nested loop, then the inner loop shall terminate, but not the outer loop.

- Now suppose you want that if the user enters a negative number, nothing really should happen. We use the *pass* statement for that.

number = input("Please enter a number: ")

while number != 5:

   print(number)

   number = input("Please enter a number: ")

   if number < 0:

      pass

Now the code shall continue to run as before – that is, the loop shall not terminate upon a negative value being entered. The *pass* statement might not seem very useful in this example; however, it comes in handy in situations where you have multiple conditional statements, and under one or more conditions, you want nothing to happen.

• Lastly, we move on to the *continue* statement. In simple words, the *continue* statement skips a particular iteration of the loop, and moves on the next one; it doesn't quit the loop altogether. This shall be better explained with a different example:

for x in range(1, 20):
    if x%2 == 0:
        continue
    print(x)

The modulus operator (%) signifies reminder. As you can see, this code prints all those values between and 20 which are not even. Essentially all values of *x* are being printed! However, there is a condition that checks to see if the number is even, and if it is, the *continue* statement is used, which skips the remaining code in the iteration, and moves on to the next iteration.

These three statements prove to be quite useful once you get your hands dirty with loops, and should come in handy quite often!

Chapter 7: Functions

Functions are another core component of programming languages, which are quite important and prove to be of great help. If you are already familiar with the concept of functions in programming, you should skip this part and move on directly to the syntax.

Functions, in a far-off way, can be considered as an extension of loops. Let's recap: The basic concept of loops of code reusability, preventing programmers from writing the same piece of code over and over again, thus making his/her life easier, conserving time and effort, and also improving code readability. Now suppose that you want a piece of code executed multiple times within a program, but you don't want it all executed in the same place, or within the same loop. What do you do?

Let me elaborate. Suppose you want five lines of asterisks to be printed five times, but you don't want them all printed at once. You want them printed at various points in the code. Logically, what you would have to do then would go something like this:

for x in range(1,5):

    *print("**")*

.

.

.

for x in range(1,5):

    *print("**")*

.

.

.

```
for x in range(1,5):

    print("*****************************************
*********")

    .

    .

    .

for x in range(1,5):

    print("*****************************************
*********")

    .

    .

    .

for x in range(1,5):

    print("*****************************************
*********")

    .

    .

    .
```

This doesn't really help us with the code reusability, does it? Essentially, what we've proven here is that loops are of help to us with code reusability only if the piece of code we want executed has to be done at the same point.

Introducing, functions. Functions are essentially blocks of code that are placed outside of the main function, and they can be called anytime through the main program, any number of times. A function is called using only a single line, so instead of having to type the same block of code five times within the main function, you type it only once, place it in a function, and simply call the function wherever you need to.

How do you do that? Let's find out.

Syntax

A function is declared like this:

def function_name():

    #block of code to be executed

And the function is called simply by this one line:

function_name()

Let's look into this in more detail with the help of an example. Suppose you want to display the table of a number up till 10, at various points throughout the code, for some reason. Here is the code for that, including the function definition and everything. This code shall also employ the concept of passing arguments to the functions, which shall be explained later.

def displayTable(number):

   for x in range(1, 11):

      *print(number, " * ", x, " = ", x*number)*

if __name__ == '__main__':

   number = input("Please enter a number:")

   displayTable(number)

   .

   .

.

number = input("Please enter a number:")

displayTable(number)

.

.

.

number = input("Please enter a number:")

displayTable(number)

.

.

.

number = input("Please enter a number:")

displayTable(number)

.

.

.

number = input("Please enter a number:")

displayTable(number)

.

.

.

As you can see, we had to write the code of displaying the table of a number only once, in a function, and we called it multiple times wherever we needed in only a single line. You can pass values to a function too. The value you pass from the main function, or wherever you currently are, to the function that you are calling, are known as arguments. The values that the function receives, which are specified in the function definition, are known as parameters. A function can receive multiple parameters or none at all. However, a function must receive exactly the same amount of arguments as specified in the function definition; else it will result in an error.

Returning values

An important thing to keep in mind is that a function is completely independent from other function within the same script. That means that it has no knowledge of the variables or lists in the other functions. This is why we need to pass arguments to functions in the first place. And this is why we often need functions to return values too.

Suppose you're writing a function which does some particular calculation on a number you send, and you want the function to return the answer, instead of displaying it, to do further processing on it, or whatever else reason. This is done like this:

def calculateSquare(number):

> *answer = number*number*
>
> *return answer*

This function returns the answer. Where you're calling the function, you'll need to store the value too, and that you will do like this:

value = calculateSquare(5)

Unlike in languages such as Java and C++, you don't need to explicitly specify if a function returns a value or not, or the type of value that it returns. Likewise, even if a function does return a value, it is not absolutely necessary that you store its value. What is necessary however, is that if you're expecting the function to return a value and call it as written above, then you should ensure that the function does indeed return a value, else the program will raise an error.

Pass by reference vs. value

In Python, values are always passed to functions by reference. This essentially means that if you pass a value to a function, and the value gets changed in the function, then the change also reflects to the original function from which this function was called. Let us elaborate this with an example:

def calculateSquare(number):

    number = number*number

if __name__ == '__main__':

    number = 2

    print(number)

    calculateSquare(number)

    print(number)

The output of the code would look like this:

2

4

Once you change the value passed in the function, it also gets changed in the calling function. Essentially, this happens because Python passes values by reference, that is, the address of the original variable is passed to the function. This is opposed to pass by value, where a copy of the variable is passed to the function, and making any change to the value in the function does not reflect to the variable in the calling function.

Global vs. local variables

The scope of a variable declared within a function is limited to that function only. This means that this variable can only be accessed within this function, but not by any other function (unless it is passed to it, of course).

Global variables are those which are declared outside of functions, and therefore they have global scope, that is, they are visible to all functions in the script, and can be accessed and modified by all of them. Here is a code that elaborates the difference:

Var1 = 2   *#global scope*

def tempFunction():

    var2 = 4   *#local scope*

if __name__ == '__main__':

    print(Var1)   *#okay*

    print(var2)   *#error!*

Function overloading

Function overloading is the concept where two functions have the same name, but different parameter types. For example, there are two functions called "printValue", but one receives a string and the other receives an integer. It is resolved at runtime which function should be called, based on the type of the argument that is passed while calling the function.

You might be familiar with this concept in C++ and Java.

However, Python does not support function overloading. This is because in function definition in Python, there is no need to define the type(s) of the argument(s) that are being passed.

Chapter 8: Files I/O

Reading from and writing to text files is also very important in programming languages. Files and databases are permanent sources of storage, so you can write something in a file, and read from it later, after exiting the code and maybe even shutting down the system. They tend to be very useful when we need to store some information permanently. For example, you may need to write a script which takes the marks of all students as user input, which would then be used by a student management system. In such a scenario, you would write a script to take the student marks as input, and write them to a file. Then the student management system can simple read the file whenever, and display the marks.

Reading from text files

The code to read all text from a text file is fairly simple. You basically open a file in read mode, and traverse and display all the lines one by one. Of course, you can do some processing on the lines too. It should go without saying that in order to read a file, the file must exist in the specified directory, otherwise an exception shall be thrown. Moreover, while we're

on the topic, one of the most common errors encountered while reading files is entering the wrong directory, or location of the file. So always be extra careful of the path that you are specifying when reading a file, not just in Python, but in any programming language!

Here's a sample code for reading a text file in Python:

```
temp_file = open('Filename.txt', 'r')

for line in temp_file:

        print(line)

temp_file.close()
```

The 'r' in this code specifies read mode. Alternatively, you can also do this:

```
with open('Filename.txt', 'r') as temp_file:

        for line in temp_file:

                print(line)
```

As you can see, in the latter block of code, there's no need to explicitly close the file; it shall close automatically once the flow of control steps out of the indent of the file opening.

Writing to text files

Writing data to text files involves a slightly bigger challenge. Basically what you need to be aware of is the fact that there are two different writing modes, when writing to a file. There's the write mode, and the append mode. If you open a file in write mode, then it shall overwrite the contents of the file if it exists. If the file doesn't exist, a new one shall be created by the specified filename. If you open a file in append mode, then whatever you write shall be added to the already existing contents of the file, if there are any. If the file doesn't exist, a new one shall be created by the specified filename.

Both modes come in handy in different situations, and which one you need depends on the scenario. Here is a sample code to write a few lines to a text file:

temp_file = open('Filename.txt', 'w')

temp_file.write("This is Python.\n")

temp_file.write("Python is a cool language.\n")

temp_file.write("Python is quite easy to learn, no?")

temp_file.close()

The 'w' in this code specifies write mode. 'a' is used to specify append mode, as in the next example. Alternatively, you can also do this:

with open('Filename.txt', 'a') as temp_file:

   temp_file.write("This is Python.\n")

   temp_file.write("Python is a cool language.\n")

   temp_file.write("Python is quite easy to learn, no?")

Conclusion

By now, you must be feeling a lot less scared than before you started reading because now you that it's so simple to learn this brilliant language. Now even though it may look tough in the beginning, it will get easier with practice, all you have to do is use the tips and techniques that we have mentioned. All of which are ready to be used at your ease. Maybe this is exactly what you needed, a full guide on what Python really is, a packed book of nothing but fruitful information.

It's an easy step by step process that will help you into getting a step closer to mastering this incredible computer language. We started from the basics and then made our way to the more specific details. This guide is for beginners who have found their passion in coding and programming, so if you really want to make an impact, now is the time!

This is a guidebook for amateurs and newbies who are willingly stepping foot in this land of programming, computers and what not. This is also a guidebook for experienced programmers who want to familiarize themselves with the language without resorting themselves to a lot of hassle and Google searches.

This guide will undoubtedly open new doors and opportunities especially since Python has become such a common language in the world of computer geniuses and computer programmers. Ever wanted to be a part of the software house?

This is your chance so grab on to it now before it's too late! Spend life doing what you love and start by Python, the ultimate programming language.

www.ingramcontent.com/pod-product-compliance
Lightning Source LLC
Chambersburg PA
CBHW061028050326
40689CB00012B/2734